FAMILY RESOURCE

Second
Edition

Growing
in
love

HomeLink Pages

Nihil Obstat
Rev. Richard L. Schaefer
Censor Deputatus

Imprimatur
✠ Most Rev. Jerome Hanus, OSB
Archbishop of Dubuque
March 19, 2002
Feast of Saint Joseph, patron of families

The nihil obstat and imprimatur are official declarations that a book or pamphlet is free of doctrinal or moral error. No implication is contained herein that those who granted the nihil obstat and imprimatur agree with the contents, opinions, or statements expressed.

ISBN: 978-0-15-901417-2
Item Number: CU0544

9 10 11 12 13 14 15 16 015016 16 15 14 13 12
Webcrafters, Inc., Madison, WI, USA; January 2012, Job# 98274

Parent Letter

Dear Parent,

You are undertaking an important step of family life–the process of sharing with your child your Catholic values concerning the inherent dignity of life and the importance of family, the morality of relationships, and human sexuality. It can be a daunting prospect, especially in today's media-saturated and often values-deprived culture, but no one is better equipped than you to carry out this most important educational task.

As you do this, you have the support of your parish community and the whole family of faith that is the Church. The *Growing in Love* program has been developed to help you, in partnership with your faith community, respond to the mandate expressed by popes and bishops, a mandate placed on all of us as members of the human family guided by the Spirit of God.

The United States bishops' document, *Human Sexuality: A Catholic Perspective for Education in Lifelong Learning*, describes three purposes for education in human sexuality:

1. To help each learner appreciate that human sexuality is a divine gift that rests at the core of the human person and enriches his or her body, emotions, and soul.

2. To help each learner appreciate the virtue of chastity as a means of directing one's sexuality to the service of love and wholeness.

3. To give each learner an appreciation of the human and Christian values that sexuality can express, and to assist the learner in following the moral norms of the Church. (*Human Sexuality*, pages 74–75)

The pages that follow were developed to assist you in the task that is yours.

Growing in Love

FAMILY RESOURCE · 4

Called to holiness and wholeness

PRINCIPAL PROGRAM CONSULTANTS

James J. DeBoy, Jr., MA
Toinette M. Eugene, PhD
Rev. Richard C. Sparks, CSP, PhD

CONSULTANTS

Sr. Jude Fitzpatrick, CHM
Pedagogy

Rev. Mark A. Ressler
Theology

Rev. Douglas O. Wathier
Theology

Daniel J. Bohle, MD (Obstetrics and Gynecology) and Anne Bohle, RN
Family Medicine and Parenting

REVIEWERS

Sr. Connie Carrigan, SSND
Religion Coordinator
Archdiocese of Miami
Miami, Florida

Mark Ciesielski
Associate Director, Office
of Continuing Christian
Education
Diocese of
Galveston-Houston
Houston, Texas

Margaret Vale DeBoy
Teacher
Arbutus Middle School
Arbutus, Maryland

Diane Dougherty
Director of Children's and
Family Catechesis
Archdiocese of Atlanta
Atlanta, Georgia

Harry J. Dudley, D. Min.
Associate Executive
Director of Faith
Formation
Archdiocese of
Indianapolis
Indianapolis, Indiana

Steven M. Ellair
Diocesan Consultant for
Elementary Catechesis
Archdiocese of Los Angeles
Los Angeles, California

Kirk Gaddy
Principal
St. Katharine Campus/
Queen of Peace School
Baltimore, Maryland

Connie McGhee
Principal
Most Holy Trinity School
San Jose, California

Barbara Minczewski
Religion Formation
Coordinator
Diocese of Davenport
Davenport, Iowa

Sr. Judy O'Brien, IHM
Rockville Centre, New York

Kenneth E. Ortega
Consultant for Media and
Curriculum
Diocese of Joliet
Joliet, Illinois

Sr. Barbara Scully, SUSC
Assistant Director of
Religious Education
Archdiocese of Boston
Randolph, Massachusetts

Rev. John H. West, STD
Theological Consultant,
Department of Education
Archdiocese of Detroit
Rector, St. John's Center for
Youth and Families
Plymouth, Michigan

OurSundayVisitor
Curriculum Division

Chapter 1

The Gift of Life

Chapter Summary

- We show respect for God's gift of life.
- Every person has gifts and limitations.
- God created people of both genders to be equal and complementary.

The Teaching Church

The mystery of what it means to be human-incarnate, embodied, and therefore sexual—is bound up in the mystery and purpose of God, who is the author of all life and love itself.

Human Sexuality, 7

Humanity was created in the image and likeness of God, "male and female" (Genesis 1:27). The creation stories in Genesis show that gender is a gift of God and that sexual identity is an essential part of the divine plan. Scripture's message is that both women and men are equal in dignity because both reflect God's own image.

The differences between men and women, their distinct characteristics and abilities, are important to what it means to be human. However, their differences are complementary and serve a most important role in creation. They are the means by which humans share in God's creative power, the power to generate new human life.

Living the Teaching

Christian parents are responsible for helping their children recognize that while each gender is distinct, neither gender is more or less deserving of dignity and respect, based upon what it can or cannot do. The message children need to hear is that all humans, of both genders, have dignity because they are created in the image of God.

- How are you affirming the special gifts, talents, and abilities of each member of your family?

- What differences, limitations, or disabilities do members of your family display?

- How do you show respect and support for every member of your family?

Getting Started

Play a game with your child. Ask your child to close his or her eyes and then open them. Tell your child to talk about the first thing he or she sees after opening his or her eyes. How is that thing a gift from God? Then you take a turn closing your eyes and talking about the first gift you see.

Talk with your child about gifts that cannot be seen, such as talents and affection. How do we know that these gifts exist? How do we use these gifts wisely?

With your child, think of ways that you can demonstrate respect for the dignity of others. Possible ways include speaking gently, listening attentively, and considering the feelings of others.

Building Understanding

Talk with your child about how the differences between the genders are part of God's plan. Reinforce the idea that the differences are good and that the physical differences exist for an important reason: bringing new life into the world.

If you, your child, or someone you know has a permanent disability or has experienced a temporary disability, such as having a broken leg or arm, talk about that disability. Discuss how having it has affected his or her life. Also discuss how learning to work around the disability has taught that person important things about other people and his or her creativity.

Continuing to Grow

With your child, review or complete the activity on page 8 of his or her book. You could also complete a list for yourself and share it with your child.

Read with your child the Bible verse on page 9 of your child's book. Make up a prayer in which you thank God for your dignity, abilities, and challenges. Conclude with the Sign of the Cross.

Review Chapter 1 of your child's book with your child. Initial the HomeLink box on page 8. Write in the box any questions or comments you may have.

Words from This Chapter

dignity *(p. 5):* Being worthy of respect. Human dignity comes from our having been created in God's image. It flows from our value as persons and not from our individual abilities, talents, or accomplishments.

disability *(p. 5):* Physical, mental, or emotional limitation or impairment; all people have both abilities and disabilities in varying degrees.

gender *(p. 6):* Being male or female.

complementary *(p. 7):* Designed to work together and help one another become more fully the persons God intended by using the physical or other gifts that the other person does not have or does not have to the same degree.

human reproductive system *(p. 7):* The parts of the body that work together to help humans conceive and give birth to children; the male and female reproductive systems are different but complementary.

When Children Ask

Why are some people "gay"? What makes a person gay?

Tell your child that people who are gay have a homosexual orientation. This means that they are sexually attracted to people of their own gender. A man who is gay is attracted to men; a woman who is gay, or lesbian, is attracted to women. No one knows for sure why some people are gay. Most people are "straight," or heterosexual. It is wrong to pick on someone for being gay or to call a person gay just because he or she may appear to be different from other people. All humans deserve respect. The Catholic Church teaches that having a homosexual orientation (experiencing oneself as gay or lesbian) is not in itself wrong, though it is disordered. However, sexual expression between homosexual persons is wrong.

Chapter 2

Called to Love

Chapter Summary
- God calls all people to a vocation of love.
- Change and growth are part of God's loving plan for creation.
- Caring for our bodies shows respect for God's plan.

The Teaching Church

Parents should pay particular attention to their children's gradual development and to their physical and psychological changes, which are decisive in the maturing of the personality.

The Truth and Meaning of Human Sexuality, #s 87–88

Change and growth are part of God's loving plan for creation. Although you may know change is good, it is not always easy to accept. The changes involved in puberty, for example, are often difficult for both parent and child. While puberty can be a particularly exciting time of life—a time of exploration and discovery—it is also a time of anguish and frustration.

At this stage of life, Christian parents must be ready to help their young adolescents understand the stages of physical and physiological development that they are about to undergo or are already undergoing—before they get too much information or misinformation from their peers or from persons who are not well-intentioned. The physiological facts about puberty should be presented in an atmosphere of calm, in a positive and reserved manner, within the framework of marriage and family.

Living the Teaching

Growth and development are part of God's plan for humans. Puberty, however, can be frightening to an uninformed child. Both boys and girls need to be accurately informed about the physical, mental, and emotional changes that accompany puberty in both genders. They need help in learning new skills to cope with the changes that come with puberty.

- How are you anticipating your child's need for information regarding puberty?
- Where do you go to inform yourself so that you can provide accurate information?
- What skills are you helping your child develop that assure them to better cope with the changes which he or she is starting to experience?

Getting Started

Talk with your child about the many ways that he or she has grown since birth. With your child, look at photographs that show his or her physical growth. Discuss your child's academic and social growth, too.

Some children approaching or already experiencing puberty may express the wish to remain children. If your child does so, point out that being anxious about present or future changes is very understandable. Reassure your child that you will help him or her understand the changes that come with growth. Remind your child that these changes will let him or her explore new parts of life that will be fun and challenging.

Talk with your child about the outcome of puberty: the ability to reproduce. Remind your child that the ability to have children is a special gift from God.

Building Understanding

Remind your child that each person is unique and that some children go through puberty sooner than others do. If your child seems unhappy with his or her growth, you may want to consult the school nurse or another medical professional.

Discuss changes in male and female bodies during puberty.

Talk about the need for increased cleanliness during puberty. With your child, work out a hygiene routine that will serve his or her needs as well as respect the needs of other family members.

Continuing to Grow

With your child, review or complete the activity on page 14 of his or her book.

Talk with your child about how light guides us in darkness. Knowledge guides us, too. Say a prayer of thanks for knowledge about life's changes. Conclude by reading the prayer on page 15 of your child's book.

Review Chapter 2 of your child's book with him or her. Initial the HomeLink box on page 14, and write your questions or comments in it.

Words from This Chapter

puberty *(p. 11):* The stage of growth during which physical, mental, and emotional changes help prepare a young person for the ability to love as an adult and also to reproduce.

fertile *(p. 11):* Able to conceive and, in women, give birth to children.

sperm cell *(p. 12):* The cell produced by the male body that joins with the female egg cell to form the first cell of a new distinct human.

egg cell *(p. 12):* The cell produced by the female body that joins with the male sperm cell to form the first cell of a new distinct human.

When Children Ask

Why do I have to shower every day?

Tell your child that the hormonal changes of puberty cause increased production of sweat and skin oils. For this reason it is important for him or her to shower or bathe daily, if possible, to shampoo frequently, and to wear clean clothing, and possibly to use a deodorant. Encourage your child to get plenty of rest, eat nutritious food, practice good cleanliness, and drink lots of water. Remind your child that underwear should be changed daily. If your child is a girl, you will need to talk to her about proper feminine hygiene and products.

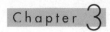

Chapter 3

The Love of Jesus

Chapter Summary

• Human sexuality is present in all relationships.

• Jesus of Nazareth had special friends.

• Jesus helps us live chaste relationships.

The Teaching Church

Jesus was a man of deep feelings, love, and commitment . . . . Likewise, we who bear the name of Christians are called to experience and express human love as whole persons—body, mind, and soul.

***Human Sexuality*, 10**

Being a woman or a man is not just incidental to who we are. Our sexuality is, as the Church tells us "a fundamental component of personality." Sexuality has an affect on our self-image, our manner of communicating with others, and the way in which we express love. Our sexuality is expressed in all our human relationships—including family, friends, and marital partners. Genital sexuality is only one way in which you experience yourself as male or female. It is this way that is reserved for Christian marriage.

Jesus himself had special friends to whom he showed care, concern, and affection. He lived chastely and did not marry, and he was a sexual being, a man who had deep feelings, which he freely expressed. His mother, his disciples, and his personal friends—Mary, Martha, Lazarus, Mary Magdalene, Peter, James, and John—all knew and experienced his friendship and love.

Living the Teaching

The Gospels tell many stories of Jesus' numerous and varied friendships. Women and men, people who were rich and poor, young and old—Jesus counted all among his friends. Having friends and being a friend require the practice of virtue. True friendships are built on honesty, trust, faithfulness, forgiveness, and love—the virtues that also sustain Christian life.

• What do you remember from Scripture about Jesus' friendships?

• What do your friendships have in common with Jesus' friendships?

• What virtues are you helping your child develop to enable him or her to be a good friend?

Getting Started

Talk with your child about his or her friends. Praise the good qualities in these children. Find out why your child feels close to these people. Encourage your child to spend time with friends and to show appreciation for them.

You may also want to discuss your own friends. Talk with your child about what brings you close to your friends. Discuss how your friends have helped you during difficult times.

Talk about differences between the genders. Explain to your child that differences in gender can help people approach problems from different angles. Talk about how such differences can also lead to deep friendships between men and women.

Building Understanding

Help your child understand why chastity is important, and encourage him or her to practice it. This could include wearing appropriate clothing and using respectful language.

With your child, evaluate media offerings, including radio programs, television shows, and movies. Talk with your child about why some programs are not suitable for young people. Guide your child in making appropriate choices.

Let your child know when you see him or her practicing a virtue. Talk about the virtues you see in him or her. Challenge your child to acquire new virtues, and praise his or her efforts.

Continuing to Grow

With your child, review or complete the activity on page 20 of his or her book. Find out why your child chose that particular virtue.

Find a quiet place to pray with your child. Hold hands with him or her, and then quietly pray together the prayer on page 21. Finish by silently thanking God for your friends.

Review Chapter 3 of your child's book with him or her. Write your questions and comments in the HomeLink box on page 20; then initial the box.

Words from This Chapter

sexuality *(p. 17):* The experience of being human, as male or female; sexuality is part of our personhood and our relationships.

virtue *(p. 18):* A habit or practice of goodness; virtues are both gifts from God and habits we can nourish through action.

chastity *(p. 19):* The virtue that helps a person express sexuality appropriately according to his or her vocation.

When Children Ask

Why can't I watch that TV show (or that movie or buy that CD) like everybody else my age?

Tell your child that it is your responsibility as a parent to evaluate the sexual content and messages that popular media convey. Your goal is to help him or her learn how to evaluate the media. One of the ways that you will help is by setting standards and guidelines for what is acceptable in your home in regard to materials of a sexual or violent nature. Explain why you find a particular TV show, movie, or piece of music unacceptable. Encourage all your children to share their views, and listen when they do so. Let them know that you will listen, even though you may not agree. Let them know that you expect the same consideration from them.

Chapter 4

Being Responsible

Chapter Summary
- We are responsible to God, ourselves, and others.
- The Christian community helps us grow in responsibility.
- We can learn about responsible love from the witness of others.

The Teaching Church

Since actions often speak louder than words, the power of parental or family example in living the Christian life should not be underestimated.

Human Sexuality, 77

"A new commandment I give you," says Jesus. "Love one another as I have loved you." Christians are responsible for answering Jesus' call to love. They are responsible to God, to themselves, and to others. As individuals, as part of a family, as members of the faith community, Christians fulfill their responsibility to love when they bear witness to the love of God in all their lives.

Saints throughout the ages have given extraordinary witness to Jesus' law of love. However, within Christian families, no witness is more important than that of parents. Actions always speak louder than words, and, in the Christian education of children, nothing is more important than the good example of loving parents.

Living the Teaching

Values and attitudes are caught more than taught. What parents do is more meaningful for children than what parents say. Values are communicated in actions. When your actions match your words, a message is clearly communicated to children and a value is transmitted.

- In what situations do your words best match your actions, and when do your actions fail to match your words?
- What kind of witness to Jesus' law of love do you give in everyday life?

Getting Started

Talk with your child about your community. Why did you choose to live there? What do you like about it? How could it be improved? Think of some projects that could improve your community, such as planting flowers in a park or visiting a senior care center. Find a way to do these projects. Or, volunteer to help with other community projects.

With your child, consider the people who help keep your community safe, such as police officers and firefighters. Describe times when you were helped by these people. Encourage your child to show appreciation to people in these and other community occupations.

Think about some of your neighbors who could use help with yard work or other household chores. With your child, offer to help these people.

Building Understanding

Discuss with your child the idea of being a witness to God's love. Help your child think of words and actions that show faith and love in difficult situations. Encourage your child to use those words and actions.

Talk about times when you have been a witness for your beliefs. How did you feel about the situation as it occurred? How did you feel about it afterward?

Share with your child the origin of his or her name. Was it given in honor of a saint or another special person? What qualities did that person have that made you want to give the name to your child?

Continuing to Grow

With your child, review or complete the activity on page 26 of his or her book. You may find it helpful to brainstorm about several admired people. Then ask your child to choose the person whose values he or she most admires.

Talk with your child about the meaning of the reflection on page 27. Help your child realize that people in our community are witnesses when they help us. And we are witnesses when we help them. Together, read the reflection.

Review Chapter 4 of your child's book with your child. Note your questions or comments in the HomeLink box on page 26, and initial it.

Words from This Chapter

responsible *(p. 23):* Answerable to God, to ourselves, and to others for our choices and actions; the quality that describes good, just, and loving actions and choices.

witness *(p. 24):* Sharing one's beliefs and values in words and actions.

When Children Ask

How do I know if I have a vocation?

Tell your child that everyone has a vocation. Often people speak of a vocation as if it were solely a call to become a priest or a religious sister or brother. However, a vocation is a call from God to live a life of love—as a single person, or within marriage, the priesthood, or religious life. Priests and religious have a special call to ministry in the Church. Using family members, friends, and parishioners as examples, talk with your child about the different ways in which adults live God's call to holiness. Tell your child that he or she may be drawn to several different paths as he or she grows older, but that the choice of a vocation is really an adult decision reached through prayer and reflection.

Chapter 5

Rules for Living

Chapter Summary

- Rules are intended to help us love.
- The Beatitudes and the Ten Commandments help us grow in love for God and others.
- We can express affection in chaste ways.
- When we sin, we must take responsibility, seek forgiveness, and make things right.

The Teaching Church

[T]he formation of conscience requires being enlightened about . . . the positive and liberating value of the moral law, and awareness both of the weakness caused by sin and the means of grace which strengthen us on our path towards the good and towards salvation.

The Truth and Meaning of Human Sexuality, #s 94–95

The Ten Commandments, Jesus' Great Commandment, and the Beatitudes help us understand what God requires of us as we answer his call to love. Responding in love, however, is made difficult by the reality of sin. Human sinfulness is present in individuals and societies. Human sinfulness and sin exerts a strong pressure on people to live their lives, including their sexuality, in ways that are contrary to the law of Christ.

Resisting the temptation to depart from the path of love requires effort. Christians who desire to remain faithful to their baptismal promises and to resist temptation will try to develop the *means* for doing so. They will strive to achieve self-knowledge and to practice self-discipline. They will look to God's commandments for guidance, and they will seek his forgiveness when they fail.

Living the Teaching

Christian parents can have an active part in the formation of their children's consciences by helping them understand God's law, especially the Ten Commandments and the Beatitudes. Teach your children how to listen for God's loving voice deep within their hearts by building the habit of daily prayer. Encourage them to reflect on how their words and deeds measure up to his expectations by stepping back from time to time and looking at their actions. Knowledge of God's law, reflection, and prayer are all necessary for moral growth.

- How do you recognize God's voice within you?
- What has most influenced the formation of your conscience?
- What are you doing to help your child form a right conscience?

Getting Started

With your child, review some of the rules of your home. Talk about whether or not the rules are effective. Should any be changed? If you don't have family rules, consider establishing some.

Talk with your child about the rules you must observe in everyday life. What is the purpose of those rules? How do they help keep order? Reinforce the idea that most rules are established for the good of many people.

Look through some of the games you have at home, or consider the sports you and your child enjoy. What rules must the players follow? How do rules make games and sports interesting? What are the penalties for not following the rules?

Building Understanding

Review with your child the Ten Commandments and the Beatitudes. (They can be found on page 32 of your child's book.) Discuss the sixth and ninth commandments and their purpose in promoting loving relationships. (See your child's book, page 29.) Talk about why the Beatitudes and commandments are useful guides. Encourage your child to use them when making choices.

Review the *Stepping Stones* feature on page 31 of your child's book. Let your child know that, like everyone, you sometimes face temptation, too. Talk about how you fight temptation. Praise your child for overcoming temptations and choosing to follow Jesus' example.

Give your child an example of loving forgiveness. The next time your child breaks a family rule, instead of immediately disciplining him or her, talk about why that rule is important.

Continuing to Grow

With your child, review or complete the activity on page 32 of your child's book.

Share with your child a story from your childhood that shows forgiveness. Then pray together the prayer on page 33 of your child's book.

Together, review through Chapter 5 of your child's book. In the HomeLink box on page 32, write your questions and comments. Add your initials.

Words from This Chapter

conscience *(p. 29):* Free will and reason working together to help us know the difference between right and wrong; a properly formed conscience helps us choose what is right.

temptation *(p. 30):* The urge or attraction to do what we know is wrong.

forgiveness *(p. 31):* An act of welcoming someone back after he or she has done wrong; acceptance of the person, not approval of the wrong behavior.

When Children Ask

Why does the Church have so many rules?

Tell your child that the Church has been in existence for a very long time, almost two thousand years. Throughout that time, the Church's role has been the same: to pass on to all generations the truth that comes from God through Jesus Christ. Because of its long experience with human nature, the Church knows that laws, rules, and guidelines are necessary for helping people understand what God requires of them. The rules that the Church establishes are given to help its members fulfill "the very necessary minimum in the spirit of prayer and moral effort, in the growth in love of God and neighbor" (Catechism, #2041). The Church's laws should not be seen as burdens to be carried, but as helps along the journey.

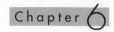

Vocations

Chapter Summary

- The Sacraments of Service—Matrimony and Holy Orders—are ways to live our vocation to love.
- All vocations call us to faithfulness.
- All vocations call us to be life-giving.

The Teaching Church

Marriage and virginity or celibacy are two ways of expressing and living the one mystery of the covenant of God with his people.

On the Family, #16

The Church's sacramental life includes two Sacraments of Service—Matrimony and Holy Orders. The Sacrament of Matrimony serves and supports the needs of Christian families, while Holy Orders serves and supports the needs of Christ's Body, the Church. Both of these sacraments enable the persons who celebrate them to live out God's call to holiness, either as a married partner or as a priest, brother, or sister. Both vocations are signs of God's relationship with people.

While marriage, priesthood, and religious life are distinctly different vocations, both call people to be life-giving and faithful. They require people to commit themselves to chastity, the virtue that helps a person express sexuality appropriately according to his or her vocation. Married people must be exclusively faithful to one another. Religious brothers, sisters, and most Catholic priests in the West must live chaste lives as celibates. The faithful fulfillment of these vocations requires sacrifice and self-denial, habits that underlie the virtue of chastity.

Living the Teaching

Christians understand that every genuine search for love, personal maturity, and interpersonal commitment involves a call to be responsible and to behave appropriately for one's particular vocation or state in life. It involves a call to chastity, a virtue that promotes self-mastery and frees love from selfishness and irresponsibility.

- How does your vocation call you to be unselfish and to take responsibility?
- As you live your own vocation, what place does the virtue of chastity have in your life?
- What are you doing to help your child learn to practice self-denial and self-mastery?

Getting Started

Talk with your child about your occupation. How did you choose it? What do you enjoy about it? How does your work serve others? With your child, consider the options he or she has for a career.

Tell your child about how you serve God, your family, and your community through your vocation. Discuss other vocations, and talk about how people who choose each vocation show love.

Tell your child about people who have served as models for you. Who were they? What made them special to you? What did you learn from them?

Building Understanding

Consider the priests or religious you know. Talk with your child about how they serve your community. How do they show their dedication to God's work? What can you and your child learn from their examples?

With your child, talk about single life. Show how the single people you know serve God in your community. Single people give life by doing God's work and helping others.

With your child, discuss married life. Using as examples you and your spouse or couples you know, talk about the rewards and challenges of married life.

Talk about how children are a special blessing from God. Share with your child the importance of protecting and nurturing human life and working to end such threats to life as abortion.

Continuing to Grow

With your child, review or complete the activity on page 38 of his or her book.

Talk with your child about how Saint Joseph followed God's plan. Pray together the prayer to Saint Joseph on page 39. Then make up your own prayer of thanks for vocations.

Review Chapter 6 with your child. Write your questions and comments in the HomeLink box on page 38 of your child's book, and initial the box.

Words from This Chapter

vocation *(p. 34):* A calling from God to live lovingly in a certain way of life.

celibate *(p. 35):* Remaining unmarried and abstaining from sexual intercourse.

virgin *(p. 35):* Never having engaged in sexual intercourse.

conception *(p. 37):* The joining of an egg cell and a sperm cell to create a new, unique human life.

abortion *(p. 37):* The death of an unborn baby; *spontaneous abortion,* or *miscarriage,* occurs when the unborn baby dies of natural causes; *direct abortion,* any intentional action taken purposely to cause the death of the unborn baby, is a serious sin.

When Children Ask

What is abortion?

While your child at this point does not need explicit information about how abortions are performed, he or she is ready to understand what abortion is and why the Church so strongly opposes it. Be clear with your child that the Church teaches that abortion is anything done to purposely end the life of an unborn baby and that it is a grave sin. Help your child understand that what society may refer to as "terminating a pregnancy" is actually ending a human life. Explain to your child that while abortion is currently legal in this country, legality does not make it right. Remind your child that at one time slavery was legal in this country, but that did not make it right. Tell him or her that there are times when standing up for what is right means taking an unpopular position and working to change the law.

Chapter 7

Friendships

Chapter Summary

- Scripture stories of friendship (Ruth and Naomi; Mary and Elizabeth; Jesus and Mary, Martha, and Lazarus and Peter) show us how to love.
- There are things we can do to build friendships.

RUTH AND NAOMI

The Teaching Church

Friendship is a sign of human and Christian solidarity.

Catechism of the Catholic Church, #1939

Scripture contains many stories of authentic friendship. The friendships between Ruth and Naomi, Mary and Elizabeth, Jesus and Peter are examples of how friends help, support, and care for one another. They are examples of authentic love and show the lengths to which friends will go when they consider the good of the other to be as important as their own good.

Educating children in right relationships is a prime responsibility of Christian parents. Wounded by human sinfulness and selfishness, children, adolescents, and young people must be helped to learn how to enter into healthy relationships with God, their families, and friends. The family is the setting where children first learn the values, attitudes, and interpersonal skills that are necessary for developing mutually satisfying, long-term relationships with others.

Living the Teaching

Children's friendships are the training grounds for important adult relationships, including marriage. Parents need to remember that the best way to teach children the ways of friendship, and especially the importance of faithfulness, self-sacrifice, and generosity to relationships, is to practice those virtues as a married couple.

- Which of your relationships are truly authentic friendships?
- What are your friendships with your spouse and others teaching your children about authentic love?

Getting Started

Talk about friendship stories from the Bible. If your child hasn't already done so, help him or her look up in the Bible the stories discussed in Chapter 7 of your child's book. Discuss how these friends are still good models for us today, even though these stories are from long ago.

Tell your child stories about your own childhood friends. Talk about how you made friends and what you and your friends enjoyed doing. If you still keep in touch with friends from your past, tell your child who those friends are. Reinforce the idea that some friendships will last a lifetime.

With your child, reflect on the idea that even Jesus had to trust people. He trusted Peter and the other disciples to carry on his work in the world. He also trusted John to care for Mary, his mother. Encourage your child to place appropriate trust in friends, too.

Building Understanding

Talk with your child about his or her friends, including their similarities and differences. Discuss how their similarities help them have fun together. Point out that the differences between your child and his or her friends will lead to an appreciation of other points of view and cultures.

Remind your child that God is a good friend, too. Encourage your child to pray often. Prayer includes telling God about joys and sorrows.

Make certain that your child understands the difference between peers and true friends. Encourage your child to respond to positive peer pressure. Help your child learn to fight against negative peer pressures.

Continuing to Grow

With your child, review or complete the activity on page 44 of his or her book.

Have your child read the proverb on page 45 of his or her book. Ask your child to interpret it; then talk about what it means to you. Hold both of your child's hands, and say together a prayer of thanks for friends, including each other.

Review Chapter 7 with your child. Add your questions, comments, and initials to the HomeLink box on page 44.

Words from This Chapter

peers *(p. 42):* People our same age who share our same circumstances.

peer pressure *(p. 42):* Positive or negative influence from our peers.

values *(p. 43):* The beliefs, moral qualities, and standards we hold and by which we live our lives.

When Children Ask

How can I get people to like me?

A key predictor of successful adaptation to adulthood is the adequacy with which a child gets along with other children. Parents need to help children develop the interpersonal skills that will enable them to form quality friendships. Tell your child that learning to get along with others is a skill that most people can learn or improve. Respect, honesty, and kindness are important in building friendships. Tell your child that making and keeping friends involves trial-and-error work. Quarrels happen, and resolving conflicts in a way that is acceptable to those involved is important. Tell your child that, unless someone is in danger of being injured, quarrels ought to be resolved by those who are quarreling. (Remember that children's solutions may be different from what an adult might provide, but that their solutions are often more creative and appropriate.)

Additional References

These resources may help you answer further questions and continue to talk with your child about sexuality and Catholic values. Some resources listed below are rooted in other Christian traditions and will need to be adapted for Catholic families or supplemented with specifically Catholic teaching.

Before You Were Born, by Henry O'Brien and Joan Lowery Nixon (Our Sunday Visitor, 1980).
    A beautifully illustrated reflection on the miracle of pregnancy and birth, simple enough for young children but useful for all ages. (K–3)

Catholic Sexual Ethics, by Ronald Lawler, Joseph Boyle Jr., and William E. May (Our Sunday Visitor, 1998).
    A sourcebook on Catholic teaching about sexuality issues. (Adult)

Contemporary Christian Morality, by Richard C. Sparks (Crossroad Publishing, 1996).
    One hundred of the most frequently asked questions regarding moral issues answered from a Christian viewpoint. (Adult)

How and When to Tell Your Kids About Sex: A Lifelong Approach to Shaping Your Child's Sexual Character, by Stanton L. Jones and Brenna B. Jones (Navarre Press, 1993).
    This guide comes from an evangelical Christian point of view and does not provide the nuances of Catholic teaching, but it offers parents of all Christian backgrounds a practical and positive approach. (Adult)

How to Talk Confidently with Your Child About Sex . . . And Appreciate Your Own Sexuality, Too, by Lenore Buth (Concordia Publishing House, 1995).
    Practical advice from a Christian perspective. (Adult)

How You Were Born, by Joanna Cole (Morrow Junior Books, 1993).
    An exploration of the beautiful process of childbirth. (K–3)

Know Your Body: A Family Guide to Sexuality and Fertility, by Charles Norris and Jean Weibel Owen (Our Sunday Visitor, 1982).
    Written from a faithful Catholic perspective, this guide is particularly helpful for discussing Natural Family Planning. (Adult)

Sex Education for Toddlers to Young Adults, by James Kenny (St. Anthony Messenger Press, 1989).
    A straight-talking guide for parents regarding many pertinent topics. (Adult)

Sex Is Not a Four-Letter Word! by Patricia Martens Miller (Crossroad Publishing, 1994).
    Practical suggestions for age-appropriate discussions between parents and children regarding sex. (Adult)

Sex Is More than a Plumbing Lesson, by Patty Stark (Preston Hollow Enterprises, 1991).
    Encourages parents to share their values and beliefs regarding sexuality with their own children in age-appropriate ways. (Adult)

Tender Love: God's Gift of Sexual Intimacy, by Bill Hybels and Rob Wilkins (Moody Press, 1993).
    A look at the spiritual side of sexuality and commitment in marriage as necessary to love in a fully human way. (Adult)

Our Sunday Visitor Curriculum Division Multimedia Resources

Catholic Values and Sexuality (video).
    Sixteen significant topics covered through drama and documentary; Parent Guide available. (Jr. High–Adult)

God's Gift (video) (produced by the Archdiocese of St. Paul-Minneapolis).
    Six videos on sexuality topics, geared to children's level of understanding. (K–6)

Growing in Love (video).
    Explores program themes and gives parents background in sharing this material with their children. (Adult)

Marriage (video) (produced by Golden Dome Productions).
    Four videos explore all stages and aspects of married life. (High School–Adult)

Movie and Video Reviews

For ratings and reviews of current and previously released films, go online to **www.usccb.org/movies**. This site, sponsored by the United States Conference of Catholic Bishops' Office for Film and Broadcasting, also features previews of movies and shows coming up on television, reviews of newly released DVDs, archived movies reviews, top 10 movie lists starting from 1965, and the Vatican top 45 movie list.

For permission to reprint copyrighted material, grateful acknowledgment is made to the following sources:

Confraternity of Christian Doctrine: Scripture texts in this work are taken from the *New American Bible with Revised New Testament and Revised Psalms* copyright © 1991, 1986, 1970 Confraternity of Christian Doctrine, Washington, D.C. and are used by permission of the copyright owner. All Rights Reserved. No part of the *New American Bible* may be reproduced in any form without permission in writing from the copyright owner.

Libreria Editrice Vaticana: Excerpts from the English translations of *Educational Guidance in Human Love: Outlines for Sex Education; The Gospel of Life: On the Value and Inviolability of Human Life (Evangelium Vitae); On the Family (Familiaris Consortio); The Truth and Meaning of Human Sexuality: Guidelines for Education Within the Family* copyright © LIBRERIA EDITRICE VATICANA. Used with permission.

United States Catholic Conference: Excerpts from *Human Sexuality: A Catholic Perspective for Education and Lifelong Learning* copyright © 1991 United States Catholic Conference, Inc., Washington, D.C. and are used by permission of the copyright owner. All Rights Reserved. No part of this document may be reproduced in any form without permission in writing from the copyright owner.

© by Our Sunday Visitor Curriculum Division, Our Sunday Visitor.

All rights reserved. No part of this publication may be reproduced or transmitted in any form or by any means, electronic or mechanical, including photocopy, recording, or any information storage and retrieval system, without permission in writing from the publisher.
> Write:
> Our Sunday Visitor Curriculum Division
> Our Sunday Visitor, Inc.
> 200 Noll Plaza, Huntington, Indiana 46750

Growing in Love is a registered trademark of Our Sunday Visitor Curriculum Division, Our Sunday Visitor, 200 Noll Plaza, Huntington, Indiana 46750.

Photography Credits
Art Resource, NY: The Pierpont Morgan Library: 8; G. Serodine: 6; **Bridgeman Art Library:** *Moses,* probably 12th century (bronze), Ashmolean Museum, Oxford, UK: 12; **Gene Plaisted/The Crosiers:** 14; **Digital Imaging Group:** 9; **Jack Holtel:** 4, 5, 10, 15, 16, 17; **PhotoEdit:** Tony Freeman: 13; **Stock Boston:** Robert E. Daemmrich: 7; **Tony Stone Images:** Tom Raymond: 11

Cover
Photo by **Jack Holtel**
Illustration by **Linda Montgomery**

4

Called to holiness and wholeness

"To live in a manner worthy of the Lord, so as to be fully pleasing, in every good work bearing fruit and growing in the knowledge of God ..."

(Colossians 1:10)

Our Sunday Visitor

Curriculum Division

www.osvcurriculum.com

Item Number: CU0544
ISBN: 978-0-15901-417-2

9 780159 014172

90000 >

Growing in Love

4

Called to holiness and wholeness

PRINCIPAL PROGRAM CONSULTANTS

James J. DeBoy, Jr., MA
Toinette M. Eugene, PhD
Rev. Richard C. Sparks, CSP, PhD

CONSULTANTS

Sr. Jude Fitzpatrick, CHM
Pedagogy

Rev. Mark A. Ressler
Theology

Rev. Douglas O. Wathier
Theology

Daniel J. Bohle, MD (Obstetrics and Gynecology) and Anne Bohle, RN
Family Medicine and Parenting

REVIEWERS

Sr. Connie Carrigan, SSND
Religion Coordinator
Archdiocese of Miami
Miami, Florida

Mark Ciesielski
Associate Director, Office of
Continuing Christian Education
Diocese of Galveston-Houston
Houston, Texas

Margaret Vale DeBoy
Teacher
Arbutus Middle School
Arbutus, Maryland

Diane Dougherty
Director of Children's and
Family Catechesis
Archdiocese of Atlanta
Atlanta, Georgia

Harry J. Dudley, D. Min.
Associate Executive Director
of Faith Formation
Archdiocese of Indianapolis
Indianapolis, Indiana

Steven M. Ellair
Diocesan Consultant for
Elementary Catechesis
Archdiocese of Los Angeles
Los Angeles, California

Kirk Gaddy
Principal
St. Katharine Campus/
Queen of Peace School
Baltimore, Maryland

Connie McGhee
Principal
Most Holy Trinity School
San Jose, California

Barbara Minczewski
Religion Formation
Coordinator
Diocese of Davenport
Davenport, Iowa

Sr. Judy O'Brien, IHM
Rockville Centre, New York

Kenneth E. Ortega
Consultant for Media and
Curriculum
Diocese of Joliet
Joliet, Illinois

Sr. Barbara Scully, SUSC
Assistant Director of Religious
Education
Archdiocese of Boston
Randolph, Massachusetts

Rev. John H. West, STD
Theological Consultant,
Department of Education
Archdiocese of Detroit
Rector, St. John's Center for
Youth and Families
Plymouth, Michigan

OurSundayVisitor

Curriculum Division

Nihil Obstat
Rev. Richard L. Schaefer
Censor Deputatus

Imprimatur
✠ Most Rev. Jerome Hanus, OSB
Archbishop of Dubuque
January 28, 2000
Feast of Saint Thomas Aquinas, Patron of Chastity and of Students

The nihil obstat and imprimatur are official declarations that a book or pamphlet is free of doctrinal or moral error. No implication is contained herein that those who granted the nihil obstat and imprimatur agree with the contents, opinions, or statements expressed.

The Ad Hoc Committee to Oversee the Use of the Catechism, National Conference of Catholic Bishops, has found this catechetical text, copyright 2001, to be in conformity with the *Catechism of the Catholic Church.*

For permission to reprint copyrighted material, grateful acknowledgment is made to the following sources:

Confraternity of Christian Doctrine: Scripture texts in this work are taken from the *New American Bible with Revised New Testament and Revised Psalms* copyright © 1991, 1986, 1970 Confraternity of Christian Doctrine, Washington, D.C. and are used by permission of the copyright owner. All Rights Reserved. No part of the *New American Bible* may be reproduced in any form without permission in writing from the copyright owner.

© 2001 by Our Sunday Visitor Curriculum Division, Our Sunday Visitor.

All rights reserved. No part of this publication may be reproduced or transmitted in any form or by any means, electronic or mechanical, including photocopy, recording, or any information storage and retrieval system, without permission in writing from the publisher.
    Write:
    Our Sunday Visitor Curriculum Division
    Our Sunday Visitor, Inc.
    200 Noll Plaza, Huntington, Indiana 46750

Growing in Love is a registered trademark of Our Sunday Visitor Curriculum Division, Our Sunday Visitor, 200 Noll Plaza, Huntington, Indiana 46750.

Photography Credits
Art Resource, NY: Giraudon: 34, 39; The Pierpont Morgan Library: 17; Tate Gallery, London: 41; **Bridgeman Art Library:** *Children dancing in the park,* Paris, July 14th, 1992 (board), by Dora Holzhandler, Private Collection: 16, 21; *Moses,* probably 12th century (bronze), Ashmolean Museum, Oxford, UK: 28; The Sermon on the Mount, illustration for *The Life of Christ,* c.1886–96 (gouache on paperboard), by James Jacques Joseph Tissot (1836–1902), Brooklyn Museum of Art, New York, USA: 29; **Catholic News Service:** 25; **Comstock:** 6, 7; **Gene Plaisted/The Crosiers:** 24, 36, 37; **Digital Imaging Group:** 16, 18, 30, 31, 43; **Susie Fitzhugh:** 13; **FPG International:** Ron Rovtar: 11; Telegraph Colour Library: 10; **France Photography:** 28, 33, 35; **Jack Holtel:** 4, 5, 9, 10, 12, 15, 22, 27, 34, 36, 40, 42; **Natural Bridges:** Robert Lentz: 24; **PhotoEdit:** Tony Freeman: 31; **Stock Boston:** Robert E. Daemmrich: 11; David J. Sams: 34; **The Stock Market:** Ariel Skelley: 4; **Tony Stone Images:** Robert E. Daemmrich: 23; Chip Henderson: 19; Dennis O'Clair: 40, 45; Tom Raymond: 23; Andy Sacks: 23; David Harry Stewart: 19

Cover
Photo by **Jack Holtel**
Illustration by **Linda Montgomery**

ISBN: 978-0-15-950666-0
Item Number: CU2101

7 8 9 10 11 12 13 14   015016 16 15 14 13 12
Webcrafters, Inc., Madison WI, USA; January 2012; Job# 97516

Growing in Love

4

Dear God our Father, thank you for the gift of life. Jesus, our brother, you taught us to respect others. Holy Spirit, help us see God in others. Amen.

The Gift of Life

Look around you. What do you see?

If you're in a classroom, you see classmates, teachers, and school materials. If you're at home, you see your family and a familiar room. What do all these things have in common?

They are all part of your life. They are all special to you. And they are all gifts from God.

Stop for a moment to think about God's gifts to you. What is your most important gift from God?

That's a hard question. Families are special. So are friends and classmates. The earth is a wonderful gift, too.

But the best gift from God is the gift of life.

God gave each person life. And God made each person special. To be alive is to be a person with **dignity**, deserving respect. This dignity can never be taken away.

We have dignity because we are humans made in God's image. We don't have to earn dignity by passing a test or by looking nice. As children of God we are all born with dignity.

God has given each of us special abilities, or talents. We should use these talents to be our best selves and to do God's work in the world.

Everyone has **disabilities**, areas in which we are challenged. These limitations can be physical, mental, or emotional. Some may affect daily living. But no matter what our disabilities are, we still have dignity.

PLANTING MIX

Different Strengths

Even though we all have abilities and disabilities, each of us has different abilities and disabilities. That's one way each person is special.

Another difference between people is **gender.** God made us as girls or boys, women or men, equal in God's eyes. Men and women can help one another become better persons.

There are some noticeable differences between men and women. For example, men are usually taller than women, although some women are taller than some men. Men's arms may be stronger than women's arms, but women's bodies are usually more flexible than men's bodies.

Catholics Believe

Men and women were made for each other.

(See Catechism, #372.)

God made men's and women's bodies different for a reason. He wanted men and women to see and appreciate the differences. God wanted men and women to know that each gender has a special part in helping create new life.

Although men's and women's bodies are different, they are **complementary**. This means that together they can bring new life into the world.

The parts of men's and women's bodies that are used to make a new life and to give birth are called the **human reproductive system**. Men's and women's reproductive systems are different but complementary.

Witness
Words

Look within yourself. From your own nature you can learn something of your Maker. The Creator of our bodies knew what he was doing.

(Saint Cyril of Jerusalem)

Giving to Each Other

Pick three people of different ages and gender. Write about the talents and gifts these people have and how they share their gifts with you.

1. _____

_____

2. _____

_____

3. _____

_____

HomeLink For Your Family

We shared this chapter. _____
We have these questions or comments:

_____

_____

_____

O LORD, you are our father;
we are the clay and you the potter:
we are all the work of your hands.

(Isaiah 64:7)

Dear God our Father, you love each of us in a special way. Jesus, help us understand the changes our bodies will go through. Holy Spirit, guide us as we grow. Amen.

Called to Love

Like this boy, you have grown in body and mind. Imagine how you will grow in the next few years!

Have you ever thought about the many ways you have grown?

Your body has gotten bigger. And you have learned to walk, talk, and take care of yourself in many ways.

At school you have grown as a student. You have studied many subjects. You have learned many skills. When you do well in school, you show yourself, your teacher, and your family that you have grown in knowledge.

You have grown in other ways, too. You know how to be kind and loving. You know how to be a friend.

God gives you gifts and talents to use now and throughout your life. He wants you to use his grace to continue to grow in body, mind, and spirit as you live out your vocation to love.

Your body is getting ready to grow in a special way. During **puberty** your body will go through the changes necessary to become an adult body.

Puberty is also a time to prepare for new kinds of loving relationships. You will grow in spirit, and you will learn to deal with the emotions that accompany love and faithfulness.

After young people have gone through puberty, they are **fertile**. Their bodies are usually able to help make new life.

As We Grow

You know that boys' bodies are different from girls' bodies. These differences become even greater during puberty.

Both boys and girls go through many changes during puberty. Because of these changes they need to eat healthful food and get more sleep and exercise so their bodies grow well. Hair begins to grow in new places on the body. Oil and sweat glands in the skin become very active, making good hygiene important. Voices deepen a little in girls and much more in boys. Girls begin to develop breasts. Most boys and girls will have a growth spurt.

Catholics
Believe

God gives people the ability and the responsibility to love.

(See Catechism, #2331.)

Each person experiences these changes at her or his own rate. Other changes during puberty prepare the human reproductive systems for adulthood.

A boy's body begins to produce **sperm cells.** These are the cells that when joined with a female **egg cell** form a new life. A man continues to produce sperm cells throughout his adult life.

A baby girl is born with many egg cells in her body. But the egg cells are not fully developed because her body isn't ready to have a baby.

During puberty the egg cells mature. About once a month, an egg cell is released in a girl's body. This means that her body is capable of having a baby.

A woman continues to release egg cells until she is between forty-five and fifty-five years of age.

Puberty and its changes bring new responsibilities. It challenges us to treat ourselves and others with respect.

Scripture
Signpost

For we are [God's] handiwork, created in Christ Jesus for the good works that God has prepared in advance.

(Ephesians 2:10)

Looking **Forward**

Fill in the lists.

What I think is great about puberty . . .

_____

_____

_____

_____

_____

_____

_____

My questions about puberty . . .

_____

_____

_____

_____

_____

_____

HomeLink For Your Family

We shared this chapter. _____

We have these questions or comments:

_____

_____

_____

Loving God, you created us and call each of us by name. May we grow in wisdom, knowledge, and grace.

(based on Isaiah 45:4)

Chapter 3

Dear God our Father, thank you for our **friends.**
Jesus, our brother, you taught us how to **treat** our friends.
Holy Spirit, help us develop many **virtues.** Amen.

The **Love** of Jesus

Think of all the special people in your life. Your parents, other family members, and teachers are all important. From them you have learned many things about life. There is another important group of people in your life—your friends.

What does a good friend do? Maybe your friend helps you with homework or spends time with you after school. Perhaps you both enjoy the same hobby. One of the most important things a friend does is help you see God in the people around you.

One of the best things you can do for a friend is to help him or her know and love God.

During a difficult situation, such as a serious illness, a friend's love can be a source of strength.

Jesus had many friends, too. He enjoyed being with his friends. He ate with them and traveled with them. And Jesus used his talents to help his friends. He told them stories to help them understand God.

From Jesus we learn how to share ourselves with our friends. We share our talents and our personalities. Males and females, boys and girls, think and act in unique ways because of the way God created them. **Sexuality** is the word used to describe these different but complementary ways of thinking and acting.

We should have friends of the other gender, as well as friends of the same gender. Friendships with people of the other gender challenge us, help us grow, and help us better understand others. These friendships also prepare us for future relationships, like dating and marriage.

In God's Time

Catholics Believe

The virtue of chastity blossoms in friendship.

(See Catechism, #2347.)

Honesty, justice, faith, and love are important qualities to have in a friendship. These qualities are also **virtues.** A virtue is a habit of doing good actions that bring us closer to God and others.

Some virtues are easier to practice than others. By continually practicing a virtue, we begin to make it a habit. For example, if you are impatient with your little brother, it will take time and effort to become patient. Pray for God's help, and practice the virtue you want to have.

Respect for Sexuality

Here are some ways to show respect for God's gift of sexuality.

- **Use respectful language when speaking about your body and the bodies of others.**

- **Don't touch the private parts of another's body.**

- **Avoid books, movies, and jokes that don't respect sexuality.**

- **Ask trusted adults any questions you have about your sexuality.**

Chastity is the virtue that helps us express our sexuality appropriately. Our sexuality, like our gender, is a gift from God. Because it is a gift, we must respect our sexuality by using it wisely and appropriately.

At your age expressing your sexuality wisely includes having both boys and girls as friends. Friends of different genders can grow to understand and enjoy each other. Understanding will help you respect others and their sexuality and learn to express your own sexuality appropriately.

Loyalty, Love, and Friendship

Write down a virtue you believe you practice.
Explain how that virtue helps your friendships.

HomeLink For Your Family

We shared this chapter. _____
We have these questions or comments:

_____

_____

_____

Lord Jesus, give us the grace to love everyone in you and for you. We give you thanks for all people, especially the friends you have given us. Love them, source of all love. Help us and our friends speak and choose and do only what is right and pleasing to you.

(based on a prayer of Saint Anselm)

Dear God our Father, you created us as part of the human community. Jesus, our Lord, help us be witnesses to your love. Holy Spirit, inspire all people to live responsibly. Amen.

Being Responsible

What does it mean to be a member of a community?

Being part of a community can be fun. It can mean going to festivals, making new friends, and learning with others.

But being part of a community means we have duties, too.

Because we belong to a community, we care about the people in it. We want them to have the things they need.

We are **responsible** members of our community when we think about what other people need and help them. When we use our talents, we are acting responsibly toward God, ourselves, and others.

When you love and care for yourself, you are honoring God. As you become the best person you can be, you contribute to the community. You learn the skills of responsible living at home and in school. Some of these skills are good communication, handling conflicts, and being aware of the rights and needs of others.

You will also learn to love responsibly. As you grow in new and different relationships, you need to recognize and use appropriate ways of showing love. This includes the responsible use of your sexuality.

When you live responsibly, those you care for are happier. Your family members and teachers are proud. And you feel good, too.

Learning from Saints

Catholics Believe

The communion of saints is a community of love and solidarity.

(See Catechism, #953.)

When you live responsibly, you are a **witness**. A witness uses words and actions to show what he or she believes.

Your family members and teachers are witnesses when they show you how to help others. There are other witnesses you can learn from, including saints and other holy people. They can teach you a lot about using God's grace to do his work and be a good person.

Saint Martin de Porres, whose name means "Martin of the poor ones," lived in Peru. He took care of many people who needed help in his community. He helped people who were sick get medical care and found ways to feed people who were hungry. Martin was a Dominican brother and took care of people of all races and religions.

Saint Martin de Porres used herbs to make healing medicines.

Saint Margaret of Scotland

Jean Donovan

Saint Margaret was the queen of Scotland, a wife, and the mother of eight children. She worked to make religion and education important values in her country. She gave time, energy, and financial support to help those who were poor.

Jean Donovan was a single woman and a missionary in El Salvador. She worked with other missionaries in the Church to help those who were poor. She loved helping the Salvadoran people. Jean stayed in El Salvador even though the country's military was in conflict with the Church and she was in danger. She was murdered in 1980.

Observe people around you, and read about the saints. They will show you how to respond to God's grace and be a witness for his love.

Witness *Words*

Do not think that saintliness comes from occupation; it depends rather on what one is. The kind of work we do does not make us holy, but we may make it so.

(Meister Eckhart)

Witnessing

Think of a person, living or deceased, whose values you admire. Write down something about that person that makes him or her a saint for you.

_____

_____

_____

_____

_____

_____

_____

_____

HomeLink For Your Family

We shared this chapter. _____

We have these questions or comments:

_____

_____

_____

Since we are surrounded by such a crowd of **witnesses**, let us **put aside** our burdens and **sins** and keep on running the race, with our eyes **on Jesus.**

(based on Hebrews 12:1–2)

Dear God our Father, thank you for guiding us in love. Jesus, you showed us that we can overcome temptation. Holy Spirit, help us follow the rules for good living. Amen.

Rules for Living

Think about life without rules. We wouldn't know how to play a game. We might not understand how to do the work our teachers assign. We would have problems at home if our families didn't know where we were or when we were coming home from a friend's house.

Rules are made because they are useful. Rules help protect us from being hurt and from hurting others. They tell us how to behave and how to relate well with other people. Rules are an attempt to put into words what we believe God wants and what will make us and our world better.

Moses received the Ten Commandments from God.

Jesus taught us the Beatitudes.

The Ten Commandments and the Beatitudes tell us how to live as loving people. For example, the sixth commandment, "You shall not commit adultery," means that we must respect God's gift of sexuality and honor family life. As adults we are faithful to our marriage vows.

The ninth commandment is "You shall not covet your neighbor's wife." For young people this relates to modesty in clothing and actions. It also means we should not be envious of other people's relationships.

"Blessed are the meek" is a Beatitude reminding us to be gentle with and respectful of other people and things. We shouldn't resort to violence or bullying.

We have a responsibility to learn and follow all the Ten Commandments and the Beatitudes. With God's grace we develop and form our **conscience**, which helps us make good decisions.

Signs of Love

Catholics Believe

The pure of heart see things as God does.

(See Catechism, #2519.)

Using our special gifts is just one way of showing our love for others.

Some of the most wonderful gifts from God are the people in our lives. God gave us family, friends, teachers, and coaches. Most of the time we enjoy being with them. There are rules about how we should act toward them. We must treat them with respect and love, just as they must treat us with respect and love. This includes not calling others names or excluding them from activities.

Treating others with respect and love also means that we use appropriate expressions of affection. Signs of affection or love should never make you or another person uncomfortable. Young people need to be modest when showing physical affection.

Sometimes we may not want to follow good rules of love and respect. Instead we may want to do something we know is wrong. This is **temptation.**

Stepping Stones

Fighting Temptation

Temptation is very common, but you don't have to give in to it. Here are some ways to fight temptation:

- **When you must make a choice, pick the choice that shows love.**

- **Consider the basic needs of yourself and others before your desires for things that you don't really need.**

- **Think about what Jesus would do. Then work to do the same.**

- **Use the Ten Commandments and the Beatitudes as guides.**

- **Pray for God's help in overcoming temptation.**

Sometimes we give in to temptation and choose to do something we know is wrong; we sin. After we sin, we may feel guilty about what we have done, especially if we have hurt others.

How can we make up for what we have done wrong? We can ask **forgiveness** of God and of those we hurt. We can celebrate the Sacrament of Reconciliation, and with God's grace we can try to make things right again.

Fill Your Heart

Inside the heart, make a collage of words and pictures that show good ways of expressing affection with respect and love.

HomeLink For Your Family

We shared this chapter. _____
We have these questions or comments:

_____

_____

_____

We give you thanks and praise,
God of love and mercy.

You are always ready to forgive.

Now is the time for your
people to turn back to you,
proclaiming the power
of your love.

*(based on Eucharistic Prayer I
for Masses of Reconciliation)*

Chapter 6

Dear God our Father, you call each of us to believe. **Jesus,** our Lord, thank you for your example. Holy Spirit, help us choose the vocation that is right for us. Amen.

Vocations

Jesus, Mary, and Joseph are good models for answering God's call to holiness. As you grow, you will make choices about your career and your **vocation.** When you make decisions, you can look at the choices others have made. Thinking about their lives can inspire you and can help you make wise choices.

Jesus served God the Father and the community. He taught people about his Father and helped those who were in need. All vocations follow the example of Jesus in different ways.

Priests and religious brothers and sisters serve God and the community in a special way through the consecrated life. These people remain **celibate** as a sign of God's kingdom yet to come and so that they can be more available to the larger community.

Single people also serve God by helping others. Everyone is single at some time, and some people choose to remain single throughout life. Single people are called to remain **virgins** before marriage. They are called to live celibate lives if they were once married but are now separated, widowed, or divorced.

As with the other vocations, married couples are called to be chaste. They express their sexuality in faithfulness to each other. They serve God and the community through their loving example and their care for their children. They expand this love to others in need.

Sacraments of Service

Catholics Believe

All are called to live chastely.

(See Catechism, #2348.)

God gives everyone the grace needed to serve him. Through the Sacraments of Holy Orders and Matrimony, God gives deacons, priests, bishops, and married couples special grace to live their vocations.

Before a man is ordained through the Sacrament of Holy Orders, he must study and prepare. He learns more about God and the Church, as well as about how to lead worship for the community. He strives to be a servant for others, remembering Jesus' example such as when he washed the apostles' feet at the Last Supper.

Most priests in the Latin Rite are required to live a celibate life. They do not get married, although some have adopted children.

The other Sacrament of Service is Matrimony. In this sacrament a man and a woman vow to commit themselves to each other and to live together and love each other for the rest of their lives.

A married couple promises to be open to new life and to welcome children into their marriage. Through **conception** the couple takes part in the creation of new life.

All human life is precious to God from its beginning. But sometimes people end the life of unborn babies on purpose. This is called **abortion**. Abortion is a serious sin.

All vocations are life-giving when the people living them serve others and promote life.

Scripture
Signpost

Serve one another through love.

(Galatians 5:13)

Ways to Serve

Write the name of a person you know and that person's vocation. Then list some of the qualities you admire about that person and his or her vocation.

HomeLink For Your Family

We shared this chapter. _____
We have these questions or comments:

_____

_____

_____

Like Saint Joseph, always faithful,
we want to share in God's loving action.
Help us hear God's call for us
as we prepare for our future.

(based on a Prayer for Vocations)

Chapter 7

Dear God our Father, you gave us people who care for us.
Jesus, our brother, you showed us how to be a good friend.
Holy Spirit, guide us in building true friendships. Amen.

Friendships

Ruth and Naomi

Friends are a special gift from God. The Bible contains stories about friends because God wants us to understand how friends help one another.

The Old Testament tells the story of Ruth and Naomi. Ruth was married to Naomi's son. After Naomi's son died, Naomi told Ruth to go back to her homeland. But Ruth would not leave her because Naomi needed her help.

The New Testament also has stories of friendship.

At the Annunciation Mary learned that her cousin Elizabeth was going to have a baby. Mary knew Elizabeth would need help, so she went to stay with her cousin.

Jesus enjoyed being with his friends. He visited Mary and Martha and taught them about God. He loved their brother, Lazarus, and raised him from the dead.

Peter was a special friend of Jesus. Because of the deep trust and faith Peter had in him, Jesus trusted Peter to lead his Church on earth.

Jesus with Peter and other disciples

From the story of Ruth and Naomi, we learn that our friends can be older or younger than we are. Friends can be of any race or religion, and they may have interests that are different from ours.

Mary and Elizabeth teach us that friends help one another. When we find out that a friend is in need, we should try to help.

Jesus shared special times with Mary, Martha, and Lazarus. Their friendship teaches us to relax and spend time with our friends. It also shows us that friends can be of the same gender or of the other gender. Jesus helped Peter become a better person. Friends should do that, too.

Love One Another

Catholics Believe

Friendship is a sign of human and Christian solidarity.

(See Catechism, #1939.)

A friend is more than a **peer.** Peers are our age and share our environment. But not all peers are friends.

Sometimes we feel **peer pressure.** This happens when our peers push us to do something. This can be good, such as when a friend encourages you to improve your grades. But it can be bad if someone pressures you to do something that is wrong, like shoplift.

A true friend would never knowingly ask you to do something wrong. If a friend does ask you to do something wrong, you have two important choices to make. The first choice is to do the right thing. The second choice is to decide whether or not this person should be your friend. You may be able to help your friend choose better. If not, you should find a better friend.

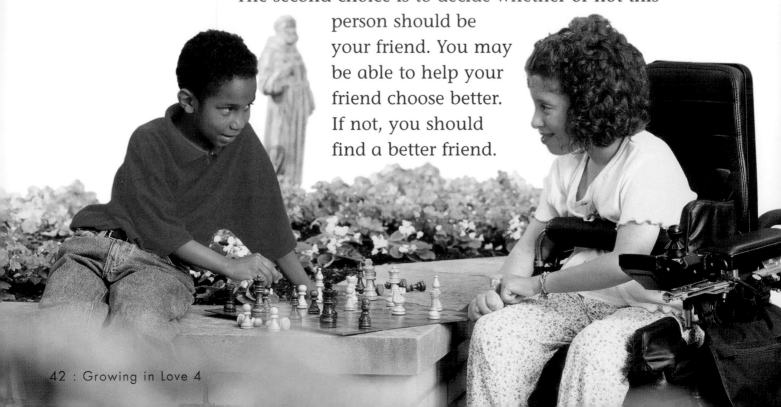

Being a Friend

Here are some ideas on how to be a good friend:

- **Choose friends who share many of your own values.**

- **Listen to your friends. Show them that you care about them.**

- **Pray for your friends.**

- **Help your friends know and do things that will bring them closer to God.**

- **Know when to ask an adult to help a friend who has a problem.**

True friends share and respect each other's good **values.** We should encourage our friends to do what is right and to have good values. We should try to lead our friends to God.

Friendship itself is a good value. Other values are honesty, fairness, respect for self and others, and compassion. Can you give examples of how people your age practice these values?

Some negative aspects of a friendship are lying, cheating, making fun of others, and bullying others. These actions damage friendships and prevent people from being the best persons they can be. Negative values can be overcome and replaced with good values, but it takes practice and determination.

My Friend

Write a letter to a friend. In the letter, describe the qualities and values you admire in your friend.

_____

_____

_____

_____

_____

_____

_____

_____

_____

HomeLink For Your Family

We shared this chapter. _____
We have these questions or comments:

_____

_____

_____

Hold a **true friend**

with both your hands.

(Nigerian Proverb)

Prayers and Resources

The Sign of the Cross
In the name of the Father,
and of the Son,
and of the Holy Spirit.
Amen.

The Lord's Prayer
Our Father, who art in heaven,
hallowed be thy name;
thy kingdom come;
thy will be done on earth as it is in heaven.
Give us this day our daily bread;
and forgive us our trespasses
as we forgive those who trespass against us;
and lead us not into temptation.
but deliver us from evil.
Amen.

Hail Mary
Hail, Mary, full of grace,
the Lord is with you!
Blessed are you among women,
and blessed is the fruit of your womb, Jesus.
Holy Mary, Mother of God,
pray for us sinners,
now and at the hour of our death.
Amen.

Glory to the Father (Doxology)

Glory to the Father, and to the Son, and to the Holy Spirit:
as it was in the beginning, is now, and will be for ever.
Amen.

Blessing Before Meals

Bless us, O Lord, and these your gifts
which we are about to receive from your goodness.
Through Christ our Lord.
Amen.

Thanksgiving After Meals

We give you thanks for all your gifts, almighty God,
living and reigning now and for ever.
Amen.

A Family Prayer

Lord our God, bless this household.
May we be blessed with health, goodness of heart,
gentleness, and the keeping of your law.
We give thanks to you,
Father, Son, and Holy Spirit,
now and for ever.
Amen.

The Great Commandment

"You shall love the Lord, your God, with all your heart, with all your being, with all your strength, and with all your mind, and your neighbor as yourself."
(Luke 10:27)

The Beatitudes

Blessed are the poor in spirit,
     for theirs is the kingdom of heaven.
Blessed are they who mourn,
     for they will be comforted.
Blessed are the meek,
     for they will inherit the land.
Blessed are they who hunger and thirst for
     righteousness,
     for they will be satisfied.
Blessed are the merciful,
     for they will be shown mercy.
Blessed are the clean of heart,
     for they will see God.
Blessed are the peacemakers,
     for they will be called children of God.
Blessed are they who are persecuted for the
     sake of righteousness,
     for theirs is the kingdom of heaven.
(Matthew 5:3–10)

The Ten Commandments

1. I am the Lord your God. You shall not have strange gods before me.
2. You shall not take the name of the Lord your God in vain.
3. Remember to keep holy the Lord's day.
4. Honor your father and your mother.
5. You shall not kill.
6. You shall not commit adultery.
7. You shall not steal.
8. You shall not bear false witness against your neighbor.
9. You shall not covet your neighbor's wife.
10. You shall not covet your neighbor's goods.